Crochet E
15 Nice Easy Baby Crochet Patterns For Beginners

All photos used in this book, including the cover photo were made available under a Attribution-ShareAlike 2.0 Generic and sourced from Flickr

Copyright 2016 by the publisher - All rights reserved.

This document is geared towards providing exact and reliable information in regards to the topic and issue covered. The publication is sold with the idea that the publisher is not required to render accounting, officially permitted, or otherwise, qualified services. If advice is necessary, legal or professional, a practiced individual in the profession should be ordered.

- From a Declaration of Principles which was accepted and approved equally by a Committee of the American Bar Association and a Committee of Publishers and Associations.

In no way is it legal to reproduce, duplicate, or transmit any part of this document in either electronic means or in printed format. Recording of this publication is strictly prohibited and any storage of this document is not allowed unless with written permission from the publisher. All rights reserved.

The information provided herein is stated to be truthful and consistent, in that any liability, in terms of inattention or otherwise, by any usage or abuse of any policies, processes, or directions contained within is the solitary and utter responsibility of the recipient reader. Under no circumstances will any legal responsibility or blame be held against the publisher for any reparation, damages, or monetary loss due to the information herein, either directly or indirectly.

Respective authors own all copyrights not held by the publisher.

The information herein is offered for informational purposes solely, and is universal as so. The presentation of the information is without contract or any type of guarantee assurance.

The trademarks that are used are without any consent, and the publication of the trademark is without permission or backing by the trademark owner. All trademarks and brands within this book are for clarifying purposes only and are the owned by the owners themselves, not affiliated with this document.

Table of content

Table of content 4
Introduction 5
Chapter 1 – Beautiful Baby Blankets 7
    The Rainbow Blanket 7
    Littlest Princess Blanket 9
    Multi-Wonder Blanket 10
Chapter 2 – Baby Hats and Beanies 12
    Little Elf Hat 12
    Adorable Striped Beanie 13
    Happy Hippy Baby Beanie 15
Chapter 3 – Adorable Baby Booties 17
    Easiest Ever Booties 17
    Little Boy Blue Booties 19
    Honey Booties 21
Chapter 4 – Safe and Sweet Baby Toys 23
    Funny Farm Finger Puppets 23
    Chirpy the Chick 25
    Sammy the Snake 27
Chapter 5 – Perfectly Baby Bibs 29
    Berry Bib 29
    Turquoise Blue Green Bib 30
    Ruffly Red Bib 32
Conclusion 34
FREE Bonus Reminder 35

Introduction

There you are, in another department store browsing through the baby section. You want something that is new and unique, but something you know your baby is going to enjoy.

All the baby blankets look so generic, but then, so do the beanies and toys. You want your baby to be warm and comfortable, but you don't want to have the latest TV star all over the top of the beanie.

You want toys for your child, but again, you want something that is cute and unique, and not something that looks like it came out of the latest television show.

But how are you going to find these things? When you only have a few options to choose from in the stores, it can start to feel limited in what you can give your child, and no one wants to feel that way.

When you can crochet, you can give your child what you want, when you want it. You aren't bound by what is on the shelves of the store, because you can give them whatever you are thinking of.

"I want to make my baby something, but I need some direction."

"I don't know if I'll make it the right size to fit my child."

"How do I know what toys to make? It seems to confusing."

If you have never made your baby crochet items before, it can feel a bit overwhelming, but don't worry. This book is going to show you a variety of patterns you can use to make your own crochet baby items, no matter what it is you want.

From blankets to beanies to toys and bibs, you will get exactly what you are looking for with this beginner book. Dive into the world of crochet with both feet, and explore your countless options time and time again.

Are you ready?

Let's get started.

Chapter 1 – Beautiful Baby Blankets

The Rainbow Blanket

Photo made by: Kate Elliott

You will need 1 ball of yarn for each of the colors you use and a size G crochet hook

Start with red, and chain a length that is 4 feet wide. Chain 1, turn, and single crochet across the row. Chain 1, turn, and single crochet back to the other side. chain 1, turn, and single crochet across the row. Chain 1, turn, and single crochet back to the other side.

Continue for a total of 10 rows.

Tie off, then join white with a slip stitch. Chain 1, and single crochet across the row. Chain 1, turn, and single crochet back to the other side. Chain 1, turn, and single crochet across the row.

Tie off, then join orange with a slip stitch. Chain 1, turn, and single crochet across the row. Chain 1, turn, and single crochet back to the other side. chain 1, turn, and single crochet across the row. Chain 1, turn, and single crochet back to the other side.

Continue for a total of 10 rows.

Tie off, then join white with a slip stitch. Chain 1, and single crochet across the row. Chain 1, turn, and single crochet back to the other side. Chain 1, turn, and single crochet across the row.

Tie off, then join yellow with a slip stitch. Chain 1, turn, and single crochet across the row. Chain 1, turn, and single crochet back to the other side. chain 1, turn, and single crochet across the row. Chain 1, turn, and single crochet back to the other side.

Continue for a total of 10 rows.

Tie off, then join white with a slip stitch. Chain 1, and single crochet across the row. Chain 1, turn, and single crochet back to the other side. Chain 1, turn, and single crochet across the row.

Continue throughout all the colors. When you have reached the last color, tie off.

Join white with a slip stitch, and work 2 rows of white border around the entire blanket. Tie off, and you are done!

Littlest Princess Blanket

Photo made by: Liz Lawley

You will need 1 ball of yarn for each of the colors you use and a size G crochet hook

Start with red, and pink a length that is 6 feet wide. Chain 1, turn, and single crochet across the row. Chain 1, turn, and single crochet back to the beginning.

Chain 1, turn, and single crochet in the first 10 stitches, then skip the next 2 stitches. Single crochet in the next 10 stitches, then skip the next 2 stitches. Single crochet in the next 10 stitches, then skip the next 2 stitches.

Continue across the row, finishing with a single crochet.

Chain 1, turn, and single crochet in the first 10 stitches, then skip the next 2 stitches. Single crochet in the next 10 stitches, then skip the next 2 stitches. Single crochet in the next 10 stitches, then skip the next 2 stitches.

Continue across the row, finishing with a single crochet.

Chain 1, turn, and single crochet across the row, this time without skipping any stitches. Follow the flow you have created, all the way across the row. Chain 1, turn, and repeat.

After you have completed 10 rows, create a stripe with the purple.

Chain 1, turn, and single crochet across the row, this time without skipping any stitches. Follow the flow you have created, all the way across the row. Chain 1, turn, and repeat.

Work 4 rows of purple, 4 rows of pink, 4 rows of purple, then work with pink for most of the blanket.

When you are happy with the length, finish with another sequence. Work 4 rows of purple, 4 rows of pink, 4 rows of purple. Finish with 10 rows of pink, then tie off.

Multi-Wonder Blanket

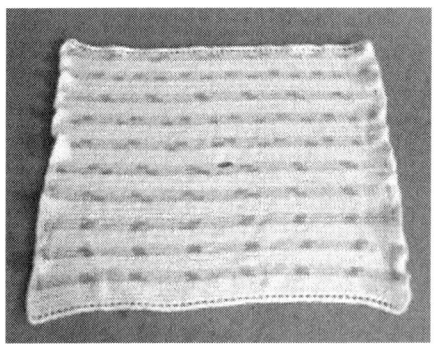

Photo made by: ~My aim is true~

You will need 1 ball of yarn for each of the colors you use and a size G crochet hook

Use a multi-colored yarn to get the self-striping effect.

Chain a length that is 5 feet wide. Chain 1, turn, and single crochet across the row. Chain 1, turn, and single crochet back to the other side. chain 1, turn, and single crochet across the row. Chain 1, turn, and single crochet back to the other side.

Continue until you have a square.

For the border, you are going to chain 10, skip 5, then join with a slip stitch. Chain 10, skip 5, then join with a slip stitch. Chain 10, skip 5, then join with a slip stitch.

Continue this around the border, then tie off.

Chapter 2 – Baby Hats and Beanies

Little Elf Hat

Photo made by: Andie712b

You will need 1 ball of yarn for each of the colors you use and a size G crochet hook

Measure around your baby's head, then chain a length that is equal to this length. Join with a slip stitch to form a ring, then single crochet back around the other side.

Chain 1, turn, and single crochet across the row, joining with a slip stitch. Continue for a total of 5 rows, then change colors.

Add the green stripe, then change to brown. Join with a slip stitch, then chain 1.

Single crochet in the first 5 stitches, then skip the next stitch. Single crochet in the next 5 stitches, then skip the next stitch. Continue around. Join with a slip stitch, chain 1, and turn.

Single crochet in the first 5 stitches, then skip the next stitch. Single crochet in the next 5 stitches, then skip the next stitch. Continue around. Join with a slip stitch, chain 1, and turn.

Use the photo as a reference to continue working your way around the entire piece. You are going to change colors every few rows, as you see in the photo, but you are also going to continue decreasing.

When you reach a fine point, tie off.

You can sew this point together and turn the hat the other way, or you can leave it raw then turn the hat the other way.

Snip off the loose ends, and your elf beanie is done!

Adorable Striped Beanie

Photo made by: PROdani0010

You will need 1 ball of yarn for each of the colors you use and a size G crochet hook

Chain 4 and join with a slip stitch to form a ring. Chain 1, and single crochet in the center of this ring 10 times. Join with a slip stitch.

Chain 2 and double crochet around the row. Join with a slip stitch, chain 2, and turn. Double crochet around the row.

Tie off, and change to the next color you wish to use. Chain 2, turn, and double crochet around the row. Join with a slip stitch, tie off, and add a new color.

You are going to continue with this pattern until the hat can cover the top of your baby's head. Now, you are ready to begin decreasing.

Chain 2, turn, and double crochet around the row. Change colors, and double crochet in the first 5 stitches, then skip the next stitch. Double crochet in the next 5 stitches, then skip the next stitch. Continue with this around the row.

Fit the hat to your baby's head, decreasing as you need to make it fit. Continue until you are happy with the size of the hat, then tie off.

Happy Hippy Baby Beanie

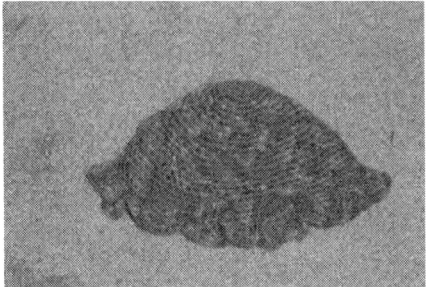

Photo made by: Ruth Temple

You will need 1 ball of yarn for each of the colors you use and a size G crochet hook

Chain 4 and join with a slip stitch to form a ring. Chain 1, and single crochet in the center of this ring 10 times. Join with a slip stitch.

Chain 1 and single crochet around the row. Join with a slip stitch, chain 1, and turn. Single crochet around the row.

Chain 1, then single crochet around the row. Join with a slip stitch, and single crochet around the other way.

You are going to continue with this pattern until the hat can cover the top of your baby's head. Now, you are ready to begin decreasing.

Chain 1, turn, and single crochet around the row. Single crochet in the first 5 stitches, then skip the next stitch. Single crochet in the next 5 stitches, then skip the next stitch. Continue with this around the row.

Fit the hat to your baby's head, decreasing as you need to make it fit. Continue until you are happy with the size of the hat, then tie off.

Join with a slip stitch.

For the border, you are going to chain 1, and single crochet in the next stitch, then double crochet in the next stitch 3 times. Single crochet in the next stitch, then double crochet in the next stitch 3 times. Single crochet in the next stitch, then double crochet in the next stitch 3 times. Single crochet in the next stitch, then double crochet in the next stitch 3 times.

Repeat this around the entire hat, joining with a slip stitch. Tie off, and you are done!

Chapter 3 – Adorable Baby Booties

Easiest Ever Booties

Photo made by: Tare Panda

You will need 1 ball of yarn for each of the colors you use and a size G crochet hook

Chain a length that is about ½ inch shorter than your baby's foot. Single crochet across the row, then around the end and across the bottom. Chain 1, and join with a slip stitch to the beginning stich in the row. Chain 1, turn, and single crochet in the chain space, then work your way down and under the row, around the front, then across the row on the top.

Join with a slip stitch. You are going to continue with this pattern around, until the piece can fit across your baby's foot. Work 3 more rows to allow for some room, then begin forming the foot.

Chain 1, and single crochet in the first 3 stitches, then skip the next stitch. Single crochet in the next 3 stitches, then skip the next stitch. Single crochet in the next 3 stitches, then skip the next stitch.

You are going to continue with this pattern around the shoe, joining with a slip stitch at the end. Chain 1, and single crochet in the first 3 stitches, then skip the next stitch. Single crochet in the next 3 stitches, then skip the next stitch. Single crochet in the next 3 stitches, then skip the next stitch.

You are going to continue with this pattern around the shoe, joining with a slip stitch at the end.

Now, continue working you way up, shaping to the foot as you work. As you shape the shoe, you are going skip decreasing around the back of the foot, but decrease around the front to form the toes.

When the bootie can fit on your baby's foot. You are ready to form the back.

Start about halfway back, and single crochet around the heel. When you get to the same point in the back, chain 1, turn, and single crochet to the beginning. Chain 1, turn, and single crochet around, this time chaining enough at the end of the row to reach across and join the other. This is going to be the strap for the bootie.

Chain 1, turn, and single crochet your way back. Continue with this pattern until you have a bootie as tall as you like, then tie off.

You can use snaps or buttons to attach top of the bootie to the other, it's up to you.

Work 1 row of single crochet around the top in the color of your choice for an embellishment, then use the same color to feed a ribbon through the base of the shoe.

Tie off, and repeat for the other side.

Little Boy Blue Booties

Photo made by: FreckledPast

You will need 1 ball of yarn for each of the colors you use and a size G crochet hook

Chain a length that is about ½ inch shorter than your baby's foot. Single crochet across the row, then around the end and across the bottom. Chain 1, and join with a slip stitch to the beginning stich in the row. Chain 1, turn, and single crochet in the chain space, then work your way down and under the row, around the front, then across the row on the top.

Join with a slip stitch. You are going to continue with this pattern around, until the piece can fit across your baby's foot. Work 3 more rows to allow for some room, then begin forming the foot.

Chain 1, and single crochet in the first 3 stitches, then skip the next stitch. Single crochet in the next 3 stitches, then skip the next stitch. Single crochet in the next 3 stitches, then skip the next stitch.

You are going to continue with this pattern around the shoe, joining with a slip stitch at the end. Chain 1, and single crochet in the first 3 stitches, then skip the next stitch. Single crochet in the next 3 stitches, then skip the next stitch. Single crochet in the next 3 stitches, then skip the next stitch.

You are going to continue with this pattern around the shoe, joining with a slip stitch at the end.

Now, continue working you way up, shaping to the foot as you work. As you shape the shoe, you are going skip decreasing around the back of the foot, but decrease around the front to form the toes.

When the bootie can fit on your baby's foot. You are ready to form the back.

Start about halfway back, and single crochet around the heel. When you get to the same point in the back, chain 1, turn, and single crochet to the beginning. Chain 1, turn, and single crochet around, this time chaining enough at the end of the row to reach across and join the other. This is going to be the strap for the bootie.

Chain 1, turn, and single crochet your way back. Continue with this pattern until you have a bootie as tall as you like, then tie off.

You can use snaps or buttons to attach top of the bootie to the other, it's up to you.

Tie off, and repeat for the other side.

Honey Booties

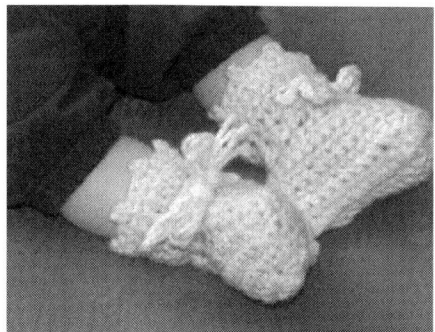

Photo made by: Jessica Merz

You will need 1 ball of yarn for each of the colors you use and a size G crochet hook

Start with yellow.

Chain a length that is about ½ inch shorter than your baby's foot. Single crochet across the row, then around the end and across the bottom. Chain 1, and join with a slip stitch to the beginning stich in the row. Chain 1, turn, and single crochet in the chain space, then work your way down and under the row, around the front, then across the row on the top.

Join with a slip stitch. You are going to continue with this pattern around, until the piece can fit across your baby's foot. Work 3 more rows to allow for some room, then begin forming the foot.

Tie off, then join blue with a slip stitch.

Chain 1, and single crochet in the first 3 stitches, then skip the next stitch. Single crochet in the next 3 stitches, then skip the next stitch. Single crochet in the next 3 stitches, then skip the next stitch.

You are going to continue with this pattern around the shoe, joining with a slip stitch at the end. Chain 1, and single crochet in the first 3 stitches, then skip the next stitch. Single crochet in the next 3 stitches, then skip the next stitch. Single crochet in the next 3 stitches, then skip the next stitch.

You are going to continue with this pattern around the shoe, joining with a slip stitch at the end.

Now, continue working you way up, shaping to the foot as you work. As you shape the shoe, you are going skip decreasing around the back of the foot, but decrease around the front to form the toes.

When the bootie can fit on your baby's foot. You are ready to form the back.

Continue with the same pattern, working your way around, simply become narrower for the top of the boot. Continue to work until you are happy with the rise, then finish with 1 row of yellow at the end.

Tie off, and repeat for the other bootie.

Chapter 4 – Safe and Sweet Baby Toys

Funny Farm Finger Puppets

Photo made by: Tracey Leigh

You will need 1 ball of yarn for each of the colors you use and a size G crochet hook

Start with the color of your choice for the animal of choice

Chain 4 and join with a slip stitch to form a ring. Chain 1, and single crochet in the center of this ring 10 times. Join with a slip stitch.

Chain 1 and single crochet around the row. Join with a slip stitch, chain 1, and turn. Single crochet around the row.

Chain 1, then single crochet around the row. Join with a slip stitch, and single crochet around the other way.

For the next row, you are going to chain 1, turn, and single crochet in the first stitch. Skip the next stitch, and single crochet in the next stitch. Skip the next stitch, and single crochet in the next stitch. Repeat around.

Join with a slip stitch.

Now, work normal crochet stitches for the duration of the project, until the length can reach down your finger. Tie off.

You are now ready to add the details:

Depending on the animal you are creating, you are going to add different details. The yarn needle and yarn will serve you well for adding eyes and mouths, but if you are making the cow, pig, or hen, you are going to need to bring your crochet hook into play a little more.

Make 2 chains for the horns on the cow, and small discs in black to add the patches. You are going to make 2 small discs for the years on the pig, and 1 chain for the comb of the chicken and the beak of the chicken and goose.

Use your yarn needle to sew the details in place, and you are done!

Chirpy the Chick

Photo made by: Tracey Leigh

You will need 1 ball of yarn for each of the colors you use and a size G crochet hook

Chain 4 and join with a slip stitch to form a ring. Chain 1, and single crochet in the center of this ring 10 times. Join with a slip stitch.

Chain 1 and single crochet around the row. Join with a slip stitch, chain 1, and turn. Single crochet around the row.

Chain 1, then single crochet around the row. Join with a slip stitch, and single crochet around the other way.

You are going to continue with this pattern for a total of 10 rows.

Now, you are ready to begin decreasing.

Chain 1, turn, and single crochet around the row. Single crochet in the first 4 stitches, then skip the next stitch. Single crochet in the next 4 stitches, then skip the next stitch. Continue with this around the row.

Work a steady decrease until you have a ball, leaving enough room at the hole to stuff. Stuff firmly, then use your yarn needle to sew the bottom closed. Set aside.

For the wings:

Chain 4 and join with a slip stitch to form a ring. Chain 1, and single crochet in the center of this ring 10 times. Join with a slip stitch.

Chain 1 and single crochet around the row. Join with a slip stitch, chain 1, and turn. Single crochet around the row.

Tie off and repeat for the other side. Sew to the body with your yarn needle, and use orange to form the beak.

If you are making this bird for a small child, embroider the eyes. If the toy is for an older child, you can use beads.

Tie off, and you are done!

Sammy the Snake

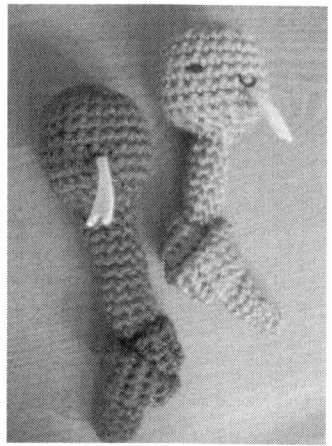

Photo made by: Arienne McCracken

You will need 1 ball of yarn for each of the colors you use and a size G crochet hook

Chain 4 and join with a slip stitch to form a ring. Chain 1, and single crochet in the center of this ring 10 times. Join with a slip stitch.

Chain 1 and single crochet around the row. Join with a slip stitch, chain 1, and turn. Single crochet around the row.

Chain 1, then single crochet around the row. Join with a slip stitch, and single crochet around the other way.

You are going to continue with this pattern for a total of 10 rows.

Now, you are ready to begin decreasing.

Chain 1, turn, and single crochet around the row. Single crochet in the first 4 stitches, then skip the next stitch. Single crochet in the next 4 stitches, then skip the next stitch. Continue with this around the row.

Work a steady decrease until you have a ball, leaving enough room at the hole to stuff. Stuff firmly, then use your yarn needle to sew the bottom closed. Set aside.

For the body:

Chain a length that is 12 stitches wide, then single crochet across the row. Chain 1, turn, and single crochet back to the beginning. Chain 1, turn, and single crochet back to the other side. Chain 1, turn, and single crochet back to the beginning.

Continue for as long as you want your snake's body to be, then taper down to a point at the bottom.

Sew the body to the head of the snake, then use your yarn needle to add the details. I chose to add felt for the tongue, but if your child is very small you may want to use the embroidery.

Snip off all loose ends, and you are done!

Chapter 5 – Perfectly Baby Bibs

Berry Bib

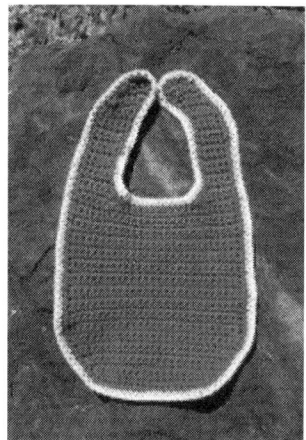

Photo made by: _StefwithanF_

You will need 1 ball of yarn for each of the colors you use and a size G crochet hook

Chain 30 and single crochet across the row. Chain 1, turn, and single crochet across the row.

Chain 1, turn, and single crochet in the first stitch 2 times, then single crochet across the row, and single crochet in the last stitch 2 times. Chain 1, turn, and single crochet in the first stitch 2 times, then single crochet across the row, and single crochet in the last stitch 2 times.

Continue to single crochet now, but do not increase anymore. Work for a total of 35 rows, then tie off.

For the arms, you are going to join with a slip stitch and single crochet 5 stitches, chain 1, turn, and single crochet across, chain 1, turn, and single crochet across. Continue for 15 rows. Tie off.

For the arms, you are going to join with a slip stitch and single crochet 5 stitches, chain 1, turn, and single crochet across, chain 1, turn, and single crochet across. Continue for 15 rows. Tie off.

Join your border color and single crochet around the entire border, joining with a slip stitch at the end. Use a snap or a button to secure in place, and you are done!

Turquoise Blue Green Bib

Photo made by: Arienne McCracken

You will need 1 ball of yarn for each of the colors you use and a size G crochet hook

Chain 30 and single crochet across the row. Chain 1, turn, and single crochet across the row.

Chain 1, turn, and single crochet in the first stitch 2 times, then single crochet across the row, and single crochet in the last stitch 2 times. Chain 1, turn, and single crochet in the first stitch 2 times, then single crochet across the row, and single crochet in the last stitch 2 times.

Continue to single crochet now, but do not increase anymore. Add 3 rows of green, then work 20 rows back in blue, then work another stripe in green.

Go back to blue.

Work for a total of 35 rows, then tie off.

For the arms, you are going to join with a slip stitch and single crochet 5 stitches, chain 1, turn, and single crochet across, chain 1, turn, and single crochet across. Continue for 15 rows. Tie off.

For the arms, you are going to join with a slip stitch and single crochet 5 stitches, chain 1, turn, and single crochet across, chain 1, turn, and single crochet across. Continue for 15 rows. Tie off.

Join your border color and single crochet around the entire border, joining with a slip stitch at the end. Use a snap or a button to secure in place, and you are done!

Ruffly Red Bib

Photo made by: Arienne McCracken

You will need 1 ball of yarn for each of the colors you use and a size G crochet hook

Chain 30 and single crochet across the row. Chain 1, turn, and single crochet across the row.

Chain 1, turn, and single crochet in the first stitch 2 times, then single crochet across the row, and single crochet in the last stitch 2 times. Chain 1, turn, and single crochet in the first stitch 2 times, then single crochet across the row, and single crochet in the last stitch 2 times.

Continue to single crochet now, but do not increase anymore. Work for a total of 35 rows, then tie off.

For the arms, you are going to join with a slip stitch and single crochet 5 stitches, chain 1, turn, and single crochet across, chain 1, turn, and single crochet across. Continue for 15 rows. Tie off.

For the arms, you are going to join with a slip stitch and single crochet 5 stitches, chain 1, turn, and single crochet across, chain 1, turn, and single crochet across. Continue for 15 rows. Tie off.

For the border:

Join with a slip stitch.

For the border, you are going to chain 1, and single crochet in the next stitch, then double crochet in the next stitch 3 times. Single crochet in the next stitch, then double crochet in the next stitch 3 times. Single crochet in the next stitch, then double crochet in the next stitch 3 times. Single crochet in the next stitch, then double crochet in the next stitch 3 times.

Repeat this around the entire piece, then finish with a button or a snap to secure, and you are done!

Conclusion

There you have it, everything you need to know about baby crochet! I hope this book inspires you to take your crochet to a whole new level, and that you are able to crochet anything and everything you like.

The patterns in this book are easy to follow, and regardless of your crochet level, you will be able to make each and every one. Have fun with crochet, and enjoy countless baby crochet projects for all occasions, no matter what the occasion is.

The world is at your fingertips with the crochet, and with these patterns, you have hour after hour of crocheting fun!

FREE Bonus Reminder

If you have not grabbed it yet, please go ahead and download your special bonus E book *"Chakras for Beginners. 7 Steps To Understand And Balance Chakras, Radiate Energy, And Strengthen Aura"*.

Simply Click the Button Below

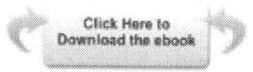

OR Go to This Page

http://lifehacksworld.com/free

BONUS #2: More Free & Discounted Books & Products

Do you want to receive more Free/Discounted Books or Products?

We have a mailing list where we send out our new Books or Products when they go free or with a discount on Amazon. Click on the link below to sign up for Free & Discount Book & Product Promotions.

=> **Sign Up for Free & Discount Book & Product Promotions** <=

OR Go to this URL

http://zbit.ly/1WBb1Ek

Printed in Great Britain
by Amazon